Restore Me

Litanies, Prayers
And Dialogues For
Lent and Easter

Craig M. Sweet

CSS Publishing Co.
Lima, Ohio

RESTORE ME

Copyright © 1994 by
The CSS Publishing Company, Inc.
Lima, Ohio

Sweet, Craig., 1956-
          Restore me: litanies, prayers, and dialogues for Lent
     and Easter / by Craig M. Sweet.
               p.   cm.
          ISBN 1-55673-700-9
          1. Lent. 2. Easter. 3. Worship programs. 4. Litanies.
     5. Prayers. I. Title
     BV85.S93   1994   93-38011
     264'.13--dc20   CIP

ISBN 1-55673-700-9

To my wife
Rev. Kathy Bueker Sweet
and our children
Zachary
and
Mara

Table Of Contents

Introduction   7

Calls To Worship For Lent   11

Benedictions For Lent   16

Common Prayers For Lent   21

Prayers Of Confession And Pardon For Lent   25

Prayers Of Dedication For Lent   34

Thanksgiving Over The Ashes   38

Calls To Worship For Easter   41

Benedictions For Easter   47

Common Prayers For Easter   52

Prayers Of Confession And Pardon For Easter   57

Prayers Of Dedication For Easter   67

Gospel Dialogues   71

Ash Wednesday
From Matthew 6:1-6, 16-21   73

Lent 1
From Matthew 4:1-11   74

Lent 2
From Mark 8:31-38   76

Lent 3
From John 2:13-22   77

Lent 4
From Luke 15:1-3, 11b-32   78

Lent 5
From John 12:20-33   80

Palm Sunday
From Matthew 21:1-11   81

Maundy Thursday
From John 13:1-17, 31-35   82

Good Friday
From John 18:1—19:42   84

Easter
From Luke 24:1-2   91

Introduction

When I first entered the local church there was a good deal of material I had learned which I couldn't wait to try out; most of which went down in the flames of inexperienced idealism. However, it has been the experiences which I witnessed as a part of the worshipping community at seminary which, with some success, I have been able to incorporate into the worship life of each congregation I have been privileged to care for. Having experienced for myself that the weekly liturgy truly is the work of the people, I have tried to bring each person in worship into a relationship with the scriptures through these prayers, litanies and dialogues.

Through the use of scripture in the planning and ordering of worship each week I have worked to bring the people into worship with the words of the Psalmist, our prayers have been drawn from and filled with the images of the scripture for the week, and we have gone forth together with words drawn from the closing chapters of our Epistle lesson.

The dialogue approach to the scripture readings I have included also reflects the understanding that the people need to become a part of the Gospel story, to make it real for them. Please be aware that any of the parts of the dialogues can be reassigned to other readers, the congregational parts can be included in the bulletin (with only the lead in lines), they may even be read by one person using a different voice or characterization for each part, or they can be used as printed. With this in mind I encourage you to look through these prayers, litanies and dialogues for those which fit with the scriptural theme you are bringing that week to worship with your people.

I pray that with the use of these resources your congregation will be drawn into a closer relationship with our Lord.

Season
Of Lent

Calls To Worship For Lent

L: Come!
P: **We come from lives of loneliness, pain and human loss
to this place at this time.**
L: Come!
P: **We come from houses without homes into worship.**
L: Come!
P: **We have come from a life of the world to life in the worship
of our God.**

L: Adonai, if you kept a record of sins, who could stand?
P: **With God there is forgiveness, and in God's Holy Word
I can find hope.**
L: Out of the depths I cry to the Lord my God for mercy;
P: **Put your hope in the Lord, for God is unfailing love and
will redeem creation from all sin.**

L: Our souls wait for the Lord; God is our help and shield.
P: **Yes, our hearts are glad in the Lord, because we trust
in God's name.**
L: O Lord, let your steadfast love be upon this congregation,
P: **Even as we gather in worship to express our hope in you.**

L: Let us sing to the Lord; let us make a joyful noise to the Rock
of our salvation!
P: **We come into God's presence with thanksgiving, making
a joyful noise to God with songs of praise!**
L: Come! Let us bow down in prayer and worship, let us kneel
before Yahweh our Maker!
P: **God is great! Adonai is sovereign and above all! Today
we have come to hear the voice of God.**

L: The Lord is my shepherd; and no longer do I want for anything.

P: Restoring my soul God leads me in the path of righteousness.

L: Even though I walk through the valley of the shadow of death, I fear no evil,

P: For you, O God, are with me; and today I have begun a habit of coming to your house.

L: I love the Lord, and I will call on God as long as I live.

P: God is gracious and righteous.

L: Return, O my soul, to your rest; for God has dealt bountifully with you.

P: I walk before the Lord in the land of the living, and believe.

L: O give thanks to the Lord, for God is good; Yahweh's steadfast love endures forever!Open to me the gates of righteousness, that I may enter through them and give thanks to the Lord.

P: The stone that the builders rejected has become the chief cornerstone. This is the Lord's doing; it is marvelous in our eyes.

L: This is the day that the Lord has made; let us rejoice and be glad in it.

P: Blessed is the one who comes in the name of the Lord. O give thanks to the Lord, for God is good, Yahweh's steadfast love endures forever.

L: This is the verdict:Light has come into the world, but people loved the darkness instead of the light.

P: God is light, in whom there is no darkness at all.

L: For God did not send the one and only Son into the world to condemn the world, but to save the world through him.

P: Come! Let us worship our God in spirit and in truth.

L: I bring you no oblation or sacrifice, my God, only a foolish and self-centered heart.

P: **I come to worship today with only a sincere desire to be your servant and walk in the path you choose for me.**

L: So I receive your love and it is channeled through me to all creation.

P: **Only in this way is my tongue set free to fully sing your praises in Holy Worship, O Lord.**

L: How great is my God, and how I love to sing God's praises!

P: **Through trial and errors, failures and successes, my God has cared for me.**

L: Sometimes through me, sometimes in spite of me, God seeks to work God's purposes in my life.

P: **How great is my God, and how I love to sing God's praises!**

L: No matter where I go, I can sense something of the power God.

P: **God's voice can be heard in all times and places. Yahweh does make his presence known.**

L: O God, in the thoughts that crowd my heart today your praises ring through in worship.

P: **In this place the power of God shines, and in this presence our praises and worship rise.**

L: By the waters of Babylon, there we sat down and wept, when we remembered Zion.

P: **How shall we sing the Lord's song in a foreign land?**

L: There the ones who captured us required us to sing, and laughed at our praise of God.

P: **Yet, even so, I now set the Lord above my highest joy as I worship in this place, the house of God.**

L: O God, my spirit flags, restore and revive me in right relationship with you.

P: **To your eternal purpose you have reinstated me that again I might know the joy and assurance of faith.**

L: And so my tongue is set free to sing, and my hands to perform your praises in worshipful life.

P: **As a child of your love I come now to praise your eternal acceptance of me in Christ.**

L: Give thanks to the Lord, for God is good; Yahweh's steadfast love endures forever!

P: **Blessed be the Lord, for whatever happens to this world God will never let me go!**

L: Love the Lord all you saints! Celebrate God and give thanks for your salvation!

P: **We cry Hosanna!, loud Hosannas! in worship. Christ comes!**

L: Because you have made God your refuge, the Most High shall be your habitation.

P: **I will say to the Lord, "My refuge and my fortress, my God in whom I trust!"**

L: When you call, God will answer; Yahweh will be present in troubled times, will rescue and honor whoever calls.

P: **With long life we will be satisfied, as the Lord shows forth our salvation!**

L: Unless God builds the house, those who work on it labor in vain.

P: **Unless God watches over the city, the sentry stays awake in vain.**

L: It is vain to eat the bread of anxious toil; for sleep is given to Yahweh's beloved.

P: **Happy are those whose lives are surrounded by children, for they are a gift of God and remind us in worship and each day of the Promise.**

L: Bless the Lord, O my soul; and all that is within me, bless God's holy name!

P: Bless the Lord, O my soul; and forget not all God's benefits!

L: Yahweh works vindication and justice for all who are oppressed. The Lord is merciful and gracious, slow to anger and abounding in steadfast love.

P: God does not deal with us according to our sins! For as the heavens are high above the earth, so great is God's love toward us! Bless the Lord, O my soul!

L: O magnify the Lord with me, and let us exalt God's name together!

P: I will bless the Lord at all times; God's praise will continually be in my mouth.

L: Look to God, and be radiant; so your faces will never be ashamed.

P: My soul makes it's boast in Adonai! O taste and see that God is Good! Happy is the one who takes refuge in God!

L: The Lord has done great things for us; We are glad!

P: When God restored the fortunes of Zion, our tongues were filled with shouts of joy!

L: May those who sow in tears, reap with shouts of joy!

P: Anyone who goes forth weeping, bearing the seed for sowing, shall come home with shouts of joy, bringing in the sheaves with them.

ALL: The Lord has done great things for us; We are glad!

Benedictions for Lent

M: Brothers and Sisters, go now to work in and for Jesus Christ alone.

P: **Christ, the treasure of our hearts, leads us on.**

M: May the love, grace and communion of God be with you now and forever. **Amen.**

M: I urge you by the love of the Spirit to pray to God.

P: **Each day as we live, our prayer will be for a life that might be an acceptable service to God.**

M: The God of peace be with you all. **Amen.**

M: Go in peace to serve God and your neighbor in all that you do.

P: **As questioning and journeying people we go out in the name of Christ.**

M: The grace of the Lord Jesus Christ and the love of God and the communion of the Holy Spirit be with you all. **Amen.**

M: Go now to greet your fellow workers in Christ Jesus.

P: **We leave here to work hard in the Lord and risk our lives for the Gospel.**

M: To the only wise God be glory forever through Jesus Christ; and may the Holy Spirit rest upon you now. **Amen.**

M: Finally, serve wholeheartedly.

P: **We know that the Lord will reward everyone for what ever good they may do.**

M: Brothers and Sisters, peace to you and love with faith from God and our Lord Jesus Christ. **Amen.**

M: There are those in this world whose lives are contrary to the teaching you have learned today, Watch out!

P: In obedience we seek only to serve Christ!

M: The grace of our Lord Jesus Christ be with you now. **Amen.**

M: All the saints send you greetings!

P: We go now to put into practice the love we have received and learned from Jesus.

M: To God be the glory and may the grace of the Lord Jesus Christ be with your spirit. **Amen.**

M: Go in peace.

P: May Jesus Christ who for our sake became obedient unto death,

M: Even death on a cross, keep you and strengthen you this night and forever. **Amen.**

M: The end of all things is at hand and above all else hold unfailing your love for one another.

P: We go now to suffer, to work under the name of God!

M: Peace to you all and to Christ be dominion for ever and ever! **Amen!**

M: Now to the one who is able to strengthen you according to the gospel and preaching of Jesus Christ,

P: To the only wise God be the glory and power for ever-more!

M: The peace of God and the grace of our Lord Jesus Christ be with you. **Amen.**

M: Be watchful, stand firm in your faith, be courageous and strong.

P: **All that we go now to do, we will do in the love of Jesus.**

M: Go now, and the grace and peace of Jesus Christ will rest upon you. **Amen.**

M Go now and in all that you do, at all times, in the Spirit pray for the Body.

P: **Christ will give us this week chances to boldly proclaim the mystery of the Gospel, and we will be ready.**

M: Peace be upon you and love with faith from God and our Lord and Savior Jesus Christ. **Amen.**

M: Now may the God of peace who brought again from the dead our Lord Jesus, by the blood of the eternal covenant;

P: **May God equip us with everything good, that we may do God's will working in us that which is pleasing in the sight of the Lord.**

M: To Jesus Christ be the honor and glory for ever and ever. **Amen.**

M: Rejoice in the Lord always, again I say rejoice! The Lord is at hand!

P: **What we have received, what we have learned and heard today, we go out now to do.**

M: And the peace of God which passes all understanding will keep your hearts and minds in Christ Jesus. **Amen.**

M: As you go about your lives this week, greet all who you meet in the name of Christ Jesus.

P: **I rejoice in the Lord greatly, for in Christ who strengthens me, I can do all things!**

M: Go now and know that God will supply your every need according to the riches of Christ Jesus. To God be the glory. The grace of our Lord Jesus Christ be with your spirit, now and always. **Amen.**

M: Finally, brothers and sisters, we cannot do anything against the truth, but only for it; and we pray for your improvement.

P: **Christ who was crucified in weakness, lives by the power of God! In Christ we are weak, but with Christ we live by the power of God!**

M: The grace of the Lord Jesus Christ, and the love of God, and the fellowship of the Holy Spirit be with you all. **Amen.**

M: Sisters and Brothers, be steadfast, immovable, always abounding in the work of the Lord, knowing that your labor is not in vain.

P: **Our Lord come! We stand in, and hold fast to, the gospel which was delivered to us.**

M: The grace of our Lord Jesus Christ be with you all. **Amen.**

M: Brothers and Sisters, God will supply every need of yours according to the riches in glory in Christ Jesus.

P: **To our God and Creator be glory for ever and ever!**

M: The grace of our Lord Jesus Christ be with your spirit. **Amen.**

M: I urge you, sisters and brothers, by our Lord Jesus Christ and by the love of the Spirit, to strive together in your prayers and work.

P: **To the One who is able to establish us according to the gospel and preaching of Jesus Christ,**

M: To the only wise God, through Jesus Christ, be the glory forever. The peace of God and the grace of Christ be with you all. **Amen.**

Common Prayers for Lent

Righteous God, searcher and reader of our hearts, create in us clean hearts and renew a right spirit within us, that through the presence and power of your Holy Spirit we each might live in the example of your Son, our Savior, Jesus Christ, in whose name we pray. **Amen.**

Sovereign God, as in the day of creation we stand naked before your almighty presence. Send out your Spirit upon us this day as we hear, interpret, and enact your Word. That we might recognize and avoid the subtle serpent of sin in our lives and so be able to live only as you choose. We pray this in the name of Jesus, our salvation. **Amen.**

Creator God, in this our time of repentance we call out for your mercy. Through your word and witness turn us back to you and to the new life Jesus Christ restored by his perfect obedience. That all the world might learn of your love. **Amen.**

Friend Jesus, teacher and guide, give to us the water of eternal life, that as it wells up within our hearts it might spill out across the earth and all might come to know the power of your love. Through the power of your Spirit we pray. **Amen.**

Prepared God, whose plans are complete in their practice, direct the choices of our lives, that in our choices we might reflect the light of your love and the care of your concern for all. We pray this in the name of Jesus, whom you sent for us in the nick of time. **Amen.**

Almighty God, whose power flashes forth from all creation, lay your hand upon us today and by your Spirit bring us out of our shells, that in all we do we might prophesy to the person of Jesus Christ, in whose name we pray. **Amen.**

Awesome God, keeper of the covenant, open our ears, lives and hearts to your Word today, that as we go about our daily lives our attitude may be the same as that of your one and only Son Jesus Christ, who out of love for us went to the cross. We pray this and all things in the precious name of Jesus. **Amen.**

Most Gracious God, look with mercy upon your family gathered here, for whom our Lord Jesus Christ was betrayed, given into sinful hands, and suffered death upon the cross. Strengthen our faith and forgive our betrayals as we enter the way of Christ's passion, through the One who lives and reigns with you and the Holy Spirit. **Amen.**

Creative God, who gave us the rainbow as a token of your covenant, send the power of your Spirit upon us, that through the touch of your hand we might hear with our whole lives your heavenly baptismal call, and so more fully be your sons and daughters. In the name of Jesus we pray. **Amen.**

O God of Abraham and Sarah, who accomplishes miracles in spite of humanity, send your Holy Spirit among us today, that as children of the promise we might renew our faith through the power of your Word; We pray this in the name of Jesus. **Amen.**

O God, judge eternal, whose foolish weakness is far greater than our human strengths and wise knowledge, we come in prayer today seeking your cleansing power for our lives, that in all things we might preach Christ and that he was crucified for all. We pray this in the righteous name of Jesus. **Amen.**

Shining God of Glory, in whose presence is all true faith and joy in believing, draw back the shades of our lives and through the work of your Spirit open our whole lives to the light of your love, for we wish to stand out in the many crowds of life as windows to your glorious light. We pray this and all things in the name of Jesus, light of the world. **Amen.**

O God of all being and freedom, we come to you in prayer today asking only to be touched by your hand, and so have our hearts and minds opened to the truth of your Word. We pray this in the name and presence of Jesus Christ. **Amen.**

Creative God, whose Word flows across creation in power, through the gift of your scriptures today catch us up in the excitement of your coming kingdom, that we might in all ways confess that Jesus Christ is Lord, to your glory and honor. We pray this in the precious name of Jesus. **Amen.**

O God of Abraham and Jacob, who let the people up out of bondage and into the promised land, send your Spirit upon us gathered here out of love for you, that as we listen to your Word we might learn how to bring others into the land of milk and honey, so in all things we would bless you, O God of Creation. In the name of Jesus we pray. **Amen.**

Covenantal God, through the words of your promise to Abraham the world was gifted with salvation in Jesus Christ. Open our ears to your Word today, that we might hear and respond to the promise of your eternal love for us. In the name of Jesus, the promised and delivered Christ. **Amen.**

O God of our ancestors, with power you spoke to Moses from the burning bush. Speak to us today from your Word with the same persuasive power, and light our hearts with the fire of your Spirit, that we, like all your servants down through time, might be able to spread the power of your love. In the name of Jesus Christ, your love incarnated we pray. **Amen.**

Gifting God, as first you gave life to creation and new life in Christ, we ask you now to give us understanding, that as we hear your Word today we might respond, not as a prodigal but with the faith and commitment of one like Paul. For we pray this in the name and presence of Jesus Christ. **Amen.**

O Holy One of Israel, who continually makes yourself known through your prophets, send your Holy Spirit upon us this morning, that we might not ignore the message of your Word, so in all we say and do we might declare your praise. In Christ we live, move, have our being and pray. **Amen.**

Prayers Of Confession
And Pardon For Lent

Righteous God, our refuge and our strength; mightily we have sinned and greatly we need your forgiveness. Not only have we listened to the subtle temptations of Satan, but we have openly worked for the Sin which you so rightly oppose. Knowing our human weakness we have come to you seeking strength for our souls and relief for our bodies. For we need to speak to Satan as Jesus did, saying "Be gone!"

Forgive us O God, purge our unrighteousness in the holy fire of your love and forge us into your pure and shining instruments.

    (silent prayer)

M: Hear the Good News: "The free gift is not like the trespass." In the name of Jesus Christ, you are forgiven!

P: Thanks be to God! In the name of Jesus Christ, you are forgiven! Amen!

O Wisdom of the Ages, you gave us minds that we might seek your truth, however, by our selfishness we have used them to create idols that excuse the comfortable ways in which we have chosen to live. Lord, we have become like Nicodemus, unable to see past the physical and into the spiritual life to which you have called us.

Forgive us our negligence. Inspire us to become seekers and speakers of truth, that we and our world, might come to know the way that leads to life eternal.

    (silent prayer)

M: And Jesus said: "Ask, and it will be given you; seek and you will find; knock, and it will be opened to you." In the name of Jesus Christ, you are forgiven!

P: Glory be to God in the highest. In the name of Jesus Christ, you are forgiven! Amen!

Redeeming God, the sin of our lives lies heavy upon our hearts. We have rejected suffering as a fact of faith. No longer do we endure in our pursuit of you, instead we have demanded drive-thru convenience and instant gratification in our prayer life. The only character we have developed is that which encourages our continued moral decline. There is little that we have done which has not disappointed you, and we are truly sorry. Forgive us, O God, and raise us up again by your grace.

    (silent prayer)

M: Hear the Good News: "While we were still powerless, at the right time Christ died for us." In the name of Jesus Christ, you are forgiven!

P: We rejoice in God through our Lord Jesus Christ! In the name of Jesus Christ, you are forgiven! Amen!

Sustaining God, stumbling along through life we have sinned and fallen from your presence. Walking in the dark we have stubbed our toes upon the unfruitful works of this world. We have judged our sisters and brothers by their appearance or stature and neglected to look upon their hearts. We have built enormous edifices to the egos that have ruled our lives. From buildings to bombs, and fortunes to feelings we have given our lives over to the designs and ideals of other human beings. Our shame lies in our sin, and our sin has been revealed to us today in your light.

Save us, O God and wake us up to the reality of life in Christ, that we might walk as children of light.

    (silent prayer)

M: Hear the Good News: "There is no condemnation for those who are in Christ Jesus." In the name of Jesus Christ, you are forgiven!

P: Glory be to God Almighty! In the name of Jesus Christ, you are forgiven! Amen!

Have mercy upon us, most merciful God. Our bodies are dead because of the sin in which we live and we are beginning to put out the fire of your Spirit. We have turned to our sisters and brothers in need and only sought to comfort them with empty phrases; no longer do we even wish to follow up our words with our actions. It has been easier to blame you for our own problems, instead of asking for your help in dealing with them. You have commanded us to "Come out!" however, we have cowered within the tombs of sin in which we have buried ourselves.

Forgive us, O God, resurrect us and raise us into the glories of your life.

(silent prayer)

M: Hear the Good News: "God who raised Christ from the dead will also give life to your mortal bodies through the Spirit, who lives in you." In the name of Jesus Christ, you are forgiven!

P: **Thanks be to the Lord Almighty. In the name of Jesus Christ, you are forgiven! Amen.**

Mighty God, sustainer of all that is and redeemer of the oppressed; forgive us. Our foremost thoughts have been how we can make our nation and ourselves equal to you. We have continually sought servants and demanded the time of others, while humbling ourselves to no one. We have accepted all the praise in our lives for ourselves and deemed that no one is as good, or as proficient as we are. We have sunk all that we are into sin, into self-centeredness.

Forgive us, O God, and enable us to truly be the Christians you created us to be.

(silent prayer)

M: And Jesus said: "I am the bread of life, whoever comes to me I will not drive away." In the name of Jesus Christ, you are forgiven!

P: **Glory, praise and honor be to God alone! In the name of Jesus Christ, you are forgiven!**

Lord Jesus, in whose hands healing has always been brought to the sick; save us and forgive us, for we are sick with sin. Our faith in you has become the business of religion and in the bureaucracy of the church we have become money-changers for society. Our faith no longer rests in you but on only those signs of the church in action around the world. We have become shallow and unstable. Forgive us; knot the cords of your love and use it to purge this sin from our hearts and create in us anew clean hearts and right spirits to your continued glory.

(silent prayer)

M: Hear the Good News: "The Lord redeems the life of servants; none of those who take refuge in God will be condemned." In the name of Jesus Christ, you are forgiven!

P: **Thanks, glory and praise be unto God! In the name of Jesus Christ, you are forgiven! Amen!**

O God, our rock and refuge, in the light of this place as we gather in prayer the manifold darkness of our lives becomes all too plain to see. We love the darkness of human power and destruction more than the light of your healing and caring. We love the darkness of self-concern and human abuse more than the light of love for you and our neighbor. We love the darkness of personal advancement and national security more than the light of the Body of Christ and eternal security. Forgive us, save us, and redeem us O God, for the further opening of your kingdom on earth.

(silent prayer)

M: Hear the Good News: "For God so loved the world that the one and only Son was given, that whoever believes in him should not perish but have eternal life." In the name of Jesus Christ, you are forgiven!

P: **By grace we have been saved through the one gift of God! In the name of Jesus Christ, you are forgiven! Amen!**

Lord Jesus, you have called us to be your servants, however all we have truly served was ourselves. We love our lives too much to risk them in uncertain ventures of faith. Human reason has grabbed our souls and wrung the last vestige of true belief from them as we watch T.V., listen to the radio, and read the newspaper. We have chosen to put our trust in those resources that can be proved on paper. Take us by the hand, re-turn us to right relationship with you, save us from ourselves.

(silent prayer)

M: And God said: "I will forgive their iniquity, and I will remember their sin no more." In the name of Jesus Christ, you are forgiven!

P: In the name of Jesus Christ, you are forgiven! Amen!

El Shaddai, compassionate and comforting God, we are sorely in need of your brooding love. Like the errant children we are, we have followed the crowd and ignored the warnings of your parental concern. We have placed status, station, and racial pride before the great commandment of your love and in our rebellion we have closed our eyes to our responsibility as stewards of this great creation. We have degraded, despoiled, and defamed your chosen servants for following your Word in their lives. Help us, O God, to stand before the world as your disciples; no matter the cost. Redeem us, and draw us closer to your loving breast.

(silent prayer)

M: The saying is sure and worthy of full acceptance, that Christ Jesus came into the world to save sinners. In the name of Jesus Christ, you are forgiven!

P: Hosanna! Hosanna in the highest! In the name of Jesus Christ, you are forgiven! Amen!

29

Saving God; redeem us from the pit of our self-serving, self-centered and self-indulgent humanity. Too easily we have fallen to the temptation of leading Jesus to the cross and following the crowd in condemnation. You have given us a world to which we must stand before you as stewards and that stewardship we have given over to greed, hate and fear. For we disfigure and maim this beautiful creation everyday with bombs, chemicals and blood. Forgive us and free us for joyful obedience.

    (silent prayer)

M: Hear the Good News: "Christ died for sins, once for all, the righteous for the unrighteous." In the name of Jesus Christ, you are forgiven!

P: **Praise God! In the name of Jesus Christ, you are forgiven! Amen!**

Redeeming God, too easily we have followed the ways of human society and not those of discipling Christianity. Not only have we denied you and laid aside the burden of your cross; but we have sought dominion over the whole world for our own gain. We have adulterated ourselves before the throne of human passions and not thrown ourselves upon the throne of grace. Save us, O God, save us from ourselves for the warring madness of humanity is upon us.

    (silent prayer)

M: Hear the Good News: "Jesus our Lord, was put to death for our trespasses and raised for our justification." In the name of Jesus Christ, you are forgiven!

P: **Thanks and praise be to God Almighty! In the name of Jesus Christ, you are forgiven! Amen!**

God of power and might, Lord of love and peace; humbly we come into your presence in prayer today, asking for your forgiveness. We have strayed from the path Jesus walked in this life and listened to the many and varied temptations of Sin. In the light of our own eyes we thought, and acted as though "might makes right," all the time forgetting that even the greatest power of our nuclear forces is weaker than your greatest weakness. Living on the brink of mutual assured destruction, we have tested you as we ought not to have done.

Forgive us, o Lord. Lead us once again into your paths of peace and let your loving light shine upon us.

(silent prayer)

M: Hear the Good News: "Whoever clings to me in love, I will deliver; I will protect the one who knows my salvation." In the name of Jesus Christ, you are forgiven!

P: In the name of Jesus Christ, you are forgiven! Glory to God! Amen!

God of grace, your love never ends; before the world was made you loved creation and after time expends you will love all that was. In the face of your love we have continued to live lives that put ourselves first. We have seen bread and wine as only food for our bodies. We have used the water of baptism to only temporarily quench our human thirst. We have misunderstood your great promises; and so approached life not as Stewards or Caretakers, but as Robber Barons and Magnates. We stretched forth our hand over creation and marred its beauty as we hacked and clawed it to pieces. Forgive us our self-indulgence. Strengthen our inner selves. Enable our continued life as your children. Make us to understand once again that only you are God.

(silent prayer)

M: And Jesus said: "Blessed is the one who comes in the name of the Lord." In the name of Jesus Christ, you are forgiven!

P: In the name of Jesus Christ, you are forgiven! Thanks be to God! Amen!

O Redeeming God, protector of all who trust in you; we have come together to hear your will for our lives, whether we agree with it or not — for we have sinned and fallen short of your glory. The lackadaisical nature of our commitment to your church makes us not even worthy to so much as gather the crumbs from under your table, yet you have given us a place at your banquet. Our chosen inability to sit still long enough to hear your response to our prayers brings us only damnation. We continually hide the lamp of our life under the basket of conformity.

Forgive us, O God. Open the eyes and ears we have closed, to the source of our salvation in Jesus Christ, and create in us your love once again.

(silent prayer)

M: Hear the Good News: "God is faithful, and will not let you be tempted beyond your strength; but will also provide the way of escape that you may be able to endure." In the name of Jesus Christ, you are forgiven!

P: As parents love their children, so God loves us and does not repay us according to our iniquities. In the name of Jesus Christ, you are forgiven! Halleluiah! Amen!

Loving Lord, all we like sheep have gone astray. Like the prodigal son we have gleefully accepted our inheritance in you and have gone and squandered it on the life of this world. By actively participating in, or passively ignoring it, we have contributed to our world's falling further away from the original goodness you created. Our weekly lives, more often than not, deny our Christian heritage; while our inner conversations with you have become in our eyes only useless monologues.

Forgive us, O Lord. Help us to live. Enable us to trust in you alone. Make us worthy of our ancestor Joshua. Save us from ourselves.

(silent prayer)

M: Hear the Good News: "If anyone is in Christ, there is a new creation; the old has passed away, the new has come." In the name of Jesus Christ, you are forgiven!

P: For our sake God made to be sin the One who knew no sin, so that we might become the righteousness of God. In the name of Jesus Christ, you are forgiven! Amen!

Mighty Redeemer, do not remember the former things, nor consider our past, for we are straining towards what lies ahead; we are pressing towards the goal of our call in Christ. And yet, we are held back by the strings of our human lives. It is still easier for us to ignore suffering, illness and depression in the world than to speak your prophetic word of release, and enact your empowering love. Our continued complicity with an unchristian political system and world has endangered our immortal souls.

Forgive us, O Lord. Redeem our lives from the pit of humanity. Enable us to only do your will. Help us to only hold true to the Gospel.

   (silent prayer)

M: And Jesus said: "I am the resurrection and the life; anyone who believes in me, though they die, yet shall they live, and whoever lives and believes in me shall never die." In the name of Jesus Christ, you are forgiven!

P: **I count everything as loss because of the surpassing worth of knowing Christ Jesus as my Lord. In the name of Jesus Christ, you are forgiven! Glory to God! Amen!**

Awesome God, companion and helper to the lonely; We are without a doubt in need of your everpresent love. For we have chosen to follow the crowd and ignore the warnings of your covenantal concern. In the arrival of Jesus we will meet not the comfy and cuddly savior we expect, but the judge and sovereign whose decision is final. The depth and intensity of our sin has blinded us to the discipleship responsibility you demand and we have become like the priests meeting Jesus on the road wishing that the noise of his passage could be lessened and so no longer disturb us.

Redeem us, restart and resurrect in us that intensity of belief and action which does categorize your chosen children.

   (silent prayer)

M: "The saying is sure and worthy of full acceptance, that Christ Jesus came into the world to save sinners." In the name of Jesus Christ, you are forgiven!

P: **Hosanna! Hosanna in the highest! In the name of Jesus Christ, you are forgiven! Amen!**

Prayers Of Dedication For Lent

Out of the storms of life, you O God, have spoken to us and for this, in the midst of our unworthiness, we praise your name and give you thanks. These tithes of our lives we dedicate to you and your purposes in this world and our lives; we pray this in the name of Jesus, the obedient one. **Amen.**

O God, eternal source of life and law. Freely we have come to give of our financial resources in total commitment to you. Receive them and take us, that you alone might be the concern of our lives. **Amen.**

Bless, O Lord, if you can, the gifts and lives we now dedicate to you; they are given in the spirit of our humanity and help us not to hold back from you, who have given us so much. In the name of Jesus, who died that we might live. **Amen.**

Eternal God, generous provider of all good gifts, we have come to bring these tithes and gifts to lay upon your altar in recognition of our deep debt to you in Jesus Christ. Take this money and the lives here today and use them as you would for what you will. **Amen.**

One and only God, Maker of heaven and earth, there is nothing that we could give which you do not already own, and yet in humble obedience we have brought these gifts and tithes that the lives they represent might become more willing to give. **Amen.**

O God, wondrous fashioner and sustainer of life; coming into your presence today we have brought this money as an offering of our lives. Accept these tithes and our lives and bless them to your continued honor and glory. **Amen.**

Almighty God, the source of all our comfort and joy, receive us and these our gifts as we dedicate them to you anew. Bless for us this time of worship and the decisions we have made here, and lead us in the path of fruitful service. **Amen.**

Enduring God, who was, is, and is to come, and still the same. We bring these firstfruits of our lives to you now and ask for your blessing upon them and your continued presence with the lives they represent; to the further glory of your purpose and presence in the world. **Amen.**

O God of Life, accept and bless to your glorious purpose of salvation these gifts and our lives. We pray in the name and power of Jesus. **Amen.**

Everliving God, thank you so much for the life and love you have blessed our lives with. As we bring this offering of our gifts and lives to you, accept and bless them that in all ways we might return to you. **Amen.**

Strong God of peace, we bring this offering of tithes to you seeking nothing for ourselves. Instead we pray that you accept it and bless each penny and each second of life represented here to the continued work of your mission. **Amen.**

O God of Abraham and Sarah, Joseph and Mary, through ancestors like these and countless others you have brought faith into our lives and given us even Jesus Christ; thank you. This day we come to return in thanks this offering of gifts and lives; take and bless it to your glory. In the name of Jesus. **Amen.**

In the name of the Lord we bring these offerings to the altar of Christ and the almighty throne of grace; that through them we might be strengthened to continue in the preparations for the return of our Lord Jesus. **Amen.**

Blessed God, look deep into our hearts and discern whether we have come to you like: Judas, craving the three hundred days wages; or Mary, who thought only of you. It is our prayer that we have brought these gifts to be like the fragrance Mary anointed you with. Consecrate them to your service and receive our lives in the promise of your love. **Amen.**

We come forward today with these gifts not so much to please ourselves or settle our consciences, but to ask your blessing upon our tithes, O Lord. Take and use these gifts and our lives for the betterment of your world and your church. Through Christ we pray. **Amen.**

Gifting God, all that we have came from you. All that we are was first a part of you. These gifts and tithes we present now are but simple tokens of the riches you first gave to us. Take our pledges and use them for the work of your church. In the precious name of Jesus we pray. **Amen.**

With bowed heads and humble hearts we bring the fruits of our labor to you, O Lord. No longer do we bring sacrifices, for in Christ you accomplished our salvation; instead we offer these gifts and our renewed lives to the glory and further growth of your kingdom. In the name of Jesus we pray. **Amen.**

Great Keeper of Promises, as we come before you now and bring these the first fruits of our lives, we give you thanks. We rejoice in all you have promised us and gifted us with. Make us worthy, and in accepting our tithe to your service, bless us that we may continue to give to others. **Amen.**

Thanksgiving Over The Ashes

M: The Lord be with you.

P: And also with you.

M: Let us pray;

Eternal God, in life, in death, in life beyond death you alone are God. You called us into being with but a word from the very dust of creation and it is into that dust that we return upon our death. We ask only that in the gift of these ashes your eternal Spirit might rest upon us in our finite humanity and remind us of our continual need for your loving grace, that in repentance we might find forgiveness, in living, faith, and in life, your everlasting love and abundant life. We pray in the precious name of Jesus, **Amen.**

Season
Of Easter

Calls To Worship For Easter

L: Adonai is my strength and my song, and Jesus Christ is my salvation!

P: **In the house of the Lord, glad songs of victory are heard, for Jesus Christ is risen!**

L: This is God's doing; it is marvelous in our eyes.

P: **This is the day which the Lord has made; Let us rejoice and be glad in it!**

L: Adonai, you have assigned me my portion and my cup; you have made my lot secure.

P: **Therefore, my heart is glad and my tongue rejoices.**

L: I will praise the Lord, who counsels me; even at night my heart instructs me.

P: **I have set the Lord always before me. I will not be shaken, and I am filled with joy as I come into God's presence now.**

L: You, O Lord, have delivered my soul from death, my eyes from tears, my feet from stumbling, that I may walk before you in the land of the living.

P: **How can I repay God for all this goodness to me? I will lift up the cup of salvation and call on the name of Jesus.**

L: Adonai, truly I am your servant; and today I come to worship you.

P: **Halleluiah! Praise the Lord!**

L: The Lord is my constant companion. There is no need that my Jesus cannot fulfill.

P: **When I feel empty and alone, Jesus fills the aching vacuum with the power of his Spirit.**

L: Jesus is ever present with me and will not leave me even if I were to flirt with death itself.

P: **My security is in God's promise and in the knowledge that the Lord will never let me go!**

L: Into your hands I commit my spirit; redeem me, O Lord, the God of truth.

P: **I will be glad and rejoice in your love, for you have not handed me over to the enemy but have set my feet in a spacious place.**

L: In you, O Lord, I have taken refuge; since you are my rock and my fortress.

P: **I trust in the Lord!**

L: Praise the Lord, O peoples, let the sound of God's praise be heard.

P: **I come into your house to worship, I have brought my offerings, my gifts, my very life to give to you.**

L: Come and listen, all you who fear God; let me tell you what God has done for me.

P: **Praise be to the Lord, who has not rejected my prayer or withheld God's love from me!**

L: Clap your hands, all you people; shout to God with the voice of triumph!

P: **How awesome is the Lord most high, the great and sovereign One over all the earth!**

L: Jesus has ascended to God amid shouts of joy!

P: **Sing praises to God, sing praises; sing praises to our King, sing praises!**

L: Clap your hands, all peoples! Shout to God with loud songs of joy!

P: **Sing praises to our ruler, sing praises with a psalm! For from the throne of grace Yahweh reigns over creation.**

L: Sing praises to God, sing praises! For God is the ruler of all the earth!

P: **For Jesus has gone up with a shout, our Lord has ascended with the sound of a trumpet!**

L: The Lord is my strength and my song; In Christ do I find my salvation!

P: I give thanks, I enter the gates of righteousness; for I have been answered and Christ is my salvation.

L: This is the day that the Lord has made; let us rejoice and be glad in it!

P: I will not die but live, and proclaim what the Lord has done!

L: In one voice we declare God's loving concern and worth to all!

P: We have seen the Lord! Christ is risen indeed!

L: In this hour of worship we come to walk in obedience to God's will.

P: Let us worship and serve our God together!

L: O God of right, you are gracious to me and hear my prayers!

P: God does hear us and we put our trust in God alone!

L: Know that God has set you apart from the world for the work of salvation.

P: The light of your countenance shines upon us, O God! In peace we come to this place to worship; for you, O God, make us dwell in safety.

L: The Lord is my constant companion and the power of Jesus' love fills the vacuum of my life.

P: God is ever present with me, in all life my security is in the promise and covenant of grace.

L: With eternal joy God touches my soul in the pain and depressions of life; That I may in all ways worship.

P: Knowing that God will never let me go frees me in faith to truly reach out to love others; and so live in love this time of praise and worship!

L: Sovereign God, I believe that you have always been with me and I know that you continue to care for me.

P: **That is why I will always sing your praises and continue to celebrate your loving presence.**

L: Through your eternally personal love you will never despise nor forsake me; no matter how terrible I feel you will always be with me.

P: **Yahweh, you are my God! I will praise and proclaim you to all the world!**

L: O sing a new song to God, who has done marvelous things!

P: **God has made known the victory and made known to all the vindication of the Lord's love and faithfulness to the house of Israel.**

L: Make a joyful noise to God, all the earth; break forth into joyous song and sing praises!

P: **Let the sea roar and the floods clap their hands; let all the world sing for joy together, for God comes!**

L: Jesus Christ is risen!

P: **Our Lord is risen indeed!**

L: We are witnesses of this and so is the Spirit whom God has given to all who have faith!

P: **In the presence and power of the risen Christ we come together in worship today!**

L: This is the day which the Lord has made; let us rejoice and be glad in it!

P: **The Lord is my strength and my song; God has become my salvation. Open the gates of righteousness, that I may enter through them and testify to Jesus Christ!**

L: I shall not die, but I shall live, and recount the deeds of Jesus. I testify that God has answered me, and become my salvation!

P: **The stone which the builders rejected has become the chief cornerstone!**

L: This is God's doing; and it is marvelous to behold!

P: **This is the day which the Lord has made; Let us rejoice and be glad in it!**

L: Why do the nations conspire, and the peoples plot in vain?

P: **The kings of the earth set themselves against Yahweh, and the rulers take counsel together against God's anointed witnesses.**

L: I will tell of the decree of the Lord, God will speak to them in anger and terrify them in fury.

P: **Now therefore O kings, be wise. Be warned O rulers of the earth!**

L: Serve Yahweh with fear, with trembling hearts adore God. Lest the Lord be angry, and you perish in the way; for God's wrath is quickly kindled.

P: **Blessed are all who take refuge in God!**

L: Sing praises to the Lord, O you of the church, and testify to God's name!

P: **To you, O Lord, I cried. To you I made my supplications, and you gave me strength and stability.**

L: You have turned my mourning into dancing, you have loosed my sackcloth and girded me with gladness.

P: **Weeping may last for the night, but joy comes in the morning!**

L: O Lord my God, I will praise you forever!

P: **My soul will praise you and never be silent!**

L: The Lord is my shepherd, I shall not be in want.

P: God restores my soul and guides me in the paths of righteousness.

L: Surely goodness and love will follow me all the days of my life,

P: And I will dwell in the house of the Lord forever.

L: The Lord is faithful in every word, and gracious in every deed.

P: Yahweh is just in all ways, and kind in every act.

L: Yahweh is near to all who call upon God in truth. God hears their cry, and saves them.

P: My mouth will speak the praise of God; let all flesh bless God's holy name forever and ever!

L: Let the peoples praise you, O God; let all the people worship you!

P: Let the nations be glad and sing for joy, for you judge the peoples with equity and guide the nations upon the earth.

L: God has blessed us; let all the ends of the earth fear God!

P: Let the peoples praise you, O God. Let all the people worship you!

L: Yahweh is here! Rejoice in the presence of the Lord!

P: You, O Most High, are exalted over all the earth!

L: Rejoice in the Lord, you who are righteous, and praise God's holy name!

P: Anyone who worships the things of this world or boasts in idols are put to shame; for Adonai reigns here, let the earth be glad!

Benedictions For Easter

M: Go out in joy to love and serve God in all that you do.

P: **We are sent in the power of Christ's resurrection! Alleluia!**

M: May the God of peace who raised to life the Great Shepherd of the sheep, make us ready to do Yahweh's will in every good thing, through Jesus Christ, to whom be glory and honor for ever and ever.

P: **Amen! Alleluia, and Alleluia!**

M: Finally, live in harmony, be sympathetic and love one another.

P: **In our pursuit of peace we have turned from evil and now go out to do good.**

M: Peace be upon you, and to Christ be the glory and the power forever and ever. **Amen.**

M: Resist evil. Stand firm in the faith.

P: **We know that our sister and brother Christians around the world are also undergoing suffering for our faith.**

M: And the God of all grace, who called you in Christ, will restore you and make you strong, firm and steadfast. To God be the power forever and ever! **Amen.**

M: Each of you must use the gifts God gave you in service to others.

P: **We go now to greet all whom we meet with the love we have received.**

M: Peace be to all who are in Christ Jesus. **Amen.**

M: Now that you have heard, spoken and sung the Word, what will you do?

P: **We will take the Word into our hearts and let the Spirit guide our lives that we may truly be servants of Jesus; Christians in more than name only!**

M: So be it! Take with you the supporting strength of God, the comforting communion of the Holy Spirit, and the knowing love of Jesus Christ. **Amen.**

M: The end is near and you have spent enough time in the past.

P: **We go now, ready to give account to the One who will judge both the living and the dead.**

M: May the love of God, the peace of Christ and the communion of the Holy Spirit be with you now. **Amen.**

M: Finally, brothers and sisters, be strong in the Lord and in God's mighty power.

P: **Having put on the full armor of God we go now to take our stand against this world and for Jesus Christ.**

M: Peace to you and love with faith from God and our Lord Jesus Christ. **Amen.**

M: Grace to all who love our Lord Jesus with undying love.

P: **In fearless declaration we go now to use our bodies and souls for the work of Christ!**

M: And so sisters and brothers in Christ, peace be upon you and love with faith from God and our Lord Jesus. **Amen.**

M: My love goes out to each of you as Christ's love works in us.

P: **A great door for effective work has been opened for our work in Jesus.**

M: Go now, Sisters and Brothers to stand firm in your faith and the grace of Our Lord Jesus Christ will be with you! **Amen.**

M: I have said these things to you who believe in the name and power of Christ that you may know that you have eternal life.

P: **With the confidence of children we know that our faith in Christ is not misplaced, for Jesus is our strength and defender.**

M: The grace, mercy, and love of Christ; risen and alive, grow in you and strengthen you to your task. **Amen.**

M: Brothers and Sisters, let no one deceive you. Test the spirits to see whether they are of God.

P: **We know that all who confess Jesus Christ as Lord and that Jesus has come in the flesh are of God; and so we are of God.**

M: Go out now, and let us love one another; for love is of God, and it is in love that the Holy Spirit rests upon you now. **Amen.**

M: By love we know that we abide in God and God in us, because we have been given the Spirit.

P: **We know that we are of God, and that the world is in the power of the evil one.**

M: Go now in the knowledge and love of God in Christ Jesus our Lord that the world too might believe. **Amen.**

M: This is the message that you have heard from the beginning, that we should love one another!

P: **We go now to love in deed and in truth.**

M: The blessing of God, the love of Jesus and the strength of the Spirit goes with you now! **Amen.**

M: That which was from the beginning, which we have heard today; this we now go to proclaim concerning the Word of life.

P: Jesus Christ is the atoning sacrifice for our sins, and not ours only but for the whole world!

M: Go now children of God, in the love of the righteous one — Jesus Christ, and be the Christians Jesus chose you to be. **Amen.**

M: Maranatha!

P: Come, Lord Jesus!

M: May your spirits be refreshed and may the grace of Jesus be upon you. **Amen.**

M: What then shall we say? If God is for us, who is against us?

P: In all things we are more than conquerors through Christ who loves us. For nothing in all creation will be able to separate us from the love of God in Christ Jesus our Lord!

M: Go and spread the good news that Christ is risen indeed, and the Holy Spirit will guide and support you in all you do. **Amen.**

M: It is done!

P: Come, Lord Jesus!

M: The grace of our Lord Jesus Christ will be with you — God's people. **Amen.**

M: Go now in the confident knowledge that God gives you strength, hope, love and peace!

P: Alleluia! and may we be the instruments of God's grace in the world where we live.

M: And may the God of peace, the Lord of life, and the Holy fire guide and support you. **Amen.**

M: We have been shown what is right and holy before the Lord.

P: Amen. Come, Lord Jesus!

M: The grace of the Lord Jesus be with all God's people. **Amen.**

M: Everything is made new in the salvation that has been given us,

P: And we stand now, ready to go forth to love, even as we have been loved in Jesus.

M: Amen! Come, Lord Jesus! **Amen!**

M: Sisters and Brothers, each day Jesus is asking us, "Do you love me?"

P: Like Peter before us we continue to say: "Yes Lord, you know that I love you," knowing that we must follow Jesus.

M: The love of God, the peace of Christ, and the fellowship of the Holy Spirit is with you now. **Amen.**

M: Grace to all who love our Lord Jesus Christ with an undying love.

P: In the strength of God Almighty we go now to do battle with the powers of this world.

M: Peace to you, and love with faith from God: Creator, Christ and Holy Spirit. **Amen.**

Common Prayers For Easter

Glorious God, sovereign eternal, enlighten the eyes of our hearts through the touch of your Spirit in our hearing of the scriptures today, that we may know the hope to which we have been called, and become living witnesses to Jesus Christ to the ends of the earth. We pray this and all things in the one and only name of Jesus Christ! **Amen!**

Yahweh, you made the world and everything in it. In the hearing and interpretation of your Word today send your Spirit upon us gathered here, that we might live and move and have our being only in you. We pray this in the name and personal presence of Jesus Christ, our resurrected Lord. **Amen.**

Father God, Judge Eternal, Mother God, lover of all souls, touch us today with the cleansing wind of your Spirit, that as we move and breathe, all of our life might reflect the grace of your eternal family. We pray this in the name of Jesus Christ, your only Child to fully understand your will and respond. **Amen.**

High and Holy God, who raised Jesus from the dead for our sakes, reach down and touch our hearts today, that in devotion to your teaching, to the fellowship, to the breaking of bread, and of prayer many more people might be added daily to those being saved. We pray this in the name of Jesus Christ, the obedient one. **Amen.**

One and only God, our refuge and our strength, cut to the chase and convict our hearts today, that in the gift of your Spirit through our baptism, we might truly be the children of your promise. We pray this in the name of Jesus Christ our Lord, who is resurrected and alive. **Amen.**

Mighty Jesus, light of the world, open our hearts and souls to the message and life of your gospel today, that as we hear God's Word today we might truly believe that you are the Christ, God's one and only Son, and that by believing we may have life in your name. **Amen.**

Powerful Creator, God of our lives, by raising Christ, you conquered the power of death and opened to us the way to eternal life. Let our celebration today raise us up too, and renew our lives by the presence of your Spirit within us. Through Jesus Christ our Lord, who lives and reigns with you and the Holy Spirit, One God, now and forever. **Amen.**

Loving God, whose jealousy has formed the responsibility of our devotion, we come in prayer this day searching for your strength and guidance, that in all we say and do we too might witness to the life, death, and resurrection of your one and only Son Jesus Christ. We pray this and all things in that precious name of Jesus. **Amen.**

Lord Jesus, whose power is that of love, enlighten the eyes of our hearts today, that we might know the hope to which you have called us, and so boldly proclaim your gospel. We pray this in your name with the help of your Spirit. **Amen.**

Shining God, whose light in Jesus Christ has illumined all creation, we come now in prayer looking into that light of love and seeking only the life you would have for us, that we might in all ways walk in the fellowship of your love. In the name of Jesus, the light of the world, we pray. **Amen.**

All powerful God, who is the answer to all mysteries, send your Spirit upon us, that in the hearing and reading of your Word the questions and troubles of our hearts will be stilled. We pray this and all things in the name of Jesus, our rock and our redeemer. **Amen.**

Shepherding God, whose love is a shelter in the storms of life, send your Spirit upon us in this time and place, that in the action of your Word we might truly know you and so live in the love of your Son Jesus Christ, in whose name we pray. **Amen.**

O God, light to the faithful and Word of life to any who seek you, we come now in prayer awaiting your guiding Spirit, that the good news of the Scripture might be opened to us and our lives to Jesus Christ, in whose name we pray. **Amen.**

Friend Jesus, you who have made known to us all that you had heard from God, be with us now in the sharing of scripture, that our lives might become enlivened by this Word and so bear abiding fruit for you that your joy may be full. We pray this in the power of your Spirit. **Amen.**

Resurrecting God, whose mighty strength was exerted in the raising of Christ and Jesus' ascension to your right hand, we simply seek in prayer today your Spirit of wisdom and revelation, that in all ways we might know Jesus Christ better, and so also the hope to which we have been called. We pray this in the glorious name of Jesus. **Amen.**

All-encompassing God, whose power and presence extend through all creation, may the presence of your Holy Spirit be especially here now to comfort us, but also to confront us with the responsibility to make your word of love become flesh in all of our actions. To your greater honor and glory we pray this in Jesus' name. **Amen.**

Dancing God, you gave us the miracle of music, help us now to put our lives in tune with your will, that true harmony might reign supreme on earth. In the name of Jesus, the obedient One, we pray. **Amen.**

O Great and Glorious God, whose power and strength can be seen in the changed lives surrounding us, we have come to be washed in the blood of the Lamb, that we might live lives of worship and service to you, thereby returning to you the love you have blessed us with. We pray this in the name of Jesus, the Great Shepherd of the sheep. **Amen.**

Penetrating God, who split the veil of the Holy of Holies when Jesus was killed for our sakes, slice through our lives and expose to our inner vision the ways in which we are to grow as your disciples, that in all we say and do the message of your word may come through. In Jesus' name. **Amen.**

O Jesus, faithful witness, firstborn from the dead and ruler of all the earth, make us into the ministers your gift on the cross destined us to be, that in all ways we might give praise, glory and honor to the One who was, is and is to be, and that your loving example might live on through us in this world and the one to come. **Amen.**

Reigning God, whose power and authority over all creation is witnessed in the resurrection of your one and only Son Jesus, we come today seeking nothing but life, life in Christ, that in our living your abundance might become known to all the world and so Christ's conquest might be complete. We pray this in the name and presence of Jesus. **Amen.**

O Christ, in whose life, death and resurrection we are justified with God, as we hear your Word for us this glorious day, may we come to recognize your living presence with us at all times, that whether in life or in death we may witness only to your Gospel. We pray this in your name. **Amen.**

Prayers Of Confession And Pardon For Easter

Holy God, before whom we kneel in awe, we confess that we have missed the mark you intended for us. We have yielded to the power of the tempter and overstepped the boundaries of our humanness. We have disobeyed you in the neglect of our neighbor. We have ignored your holy calling and misused the means of your grace. Our sin cries out for your forgiving touch!

Lord, have mercy on us. Christ, have mercy on us. Lord, have mercy on us and grant us your peace.

(silent prayer)

M: Hear the good news: "There is no sin so terrible that God's love cannot overcome and forgive." In the name of Jesus Christ, you are forgiven!

P: **Praise be to God who has given us new birth into a living hope through the resurrection of Jesus Christ! In the name of Jesus Christ, you are forgiven! Amen!**

Gracious God, forgive us. We have walked with your one and only Son, Jesus has supported, even carried us in troubled times and we have refused to acknowledge his presence. We have been foolish and slow of heart, for we have heard the scriptures and their interpretation and we have continued to refuse to believe in the power of resurrection — for it is not humanly possible. And that is the point isn't it, O Lord, new life is something we cannot attain through our own works but only through Jesus and his one perfect gift of love. Save us from this corrupt generation and add us into your family.

(silent prayer)

M: Hear the good news: "It was not with perishable things like silver or gold that you were saved, but with the precious blood of Christ." In the name of Jesus Christ, you are forgiven!

P: **The word of the Lord stands forever! Praise be to God Almighty! In the name of Jesus Christ, you are forgiven! Amen!**

Shepherding God, all we like sheep have gone astray. We have become the hired hand and abandoned your sheep in the face of Satan's attack. We have been more concerned for our own lives than for those whom you have placed in our care. We have come into your church like thieves and robbers as we have refused to enter through the gate: Jesus. Our goal has been to control and possess power over our brothers and sisters. Our interest has been ourselves and we have been shamed by the example of Christ. Forgive us, O God and enable us to truly hear the voice of our Shepherd and Savior, Jesus Christ.

    (silent prayer)

M: Hear the good news: "Jesus bore our sins in his body on the cross; by his wounds you are healed." In the name of Jesus Christ, you are forgiven!

P: Praise be to God Almighty! In the name of Jesus Christ, you are forgiven! Halleluiah!

O God, shield of our mothers and fathers, we have fallen far short of the plans you have had for our lives. To this point we acknowledge the disappointment our lives have become, however, we intend to change, truly we do. No longer shall we stone your prophets. No longer will we fall asleep in the presence of Jesus. Never again will we reject your Cornerstone. Maybe you have heard it all before, but this time it's different. No longer will we attempt to be yours through our own plans and schemes, but only through Jesus and your Holy Spirit.

    Like newborn babies craving pure spiritual milk we have come seeking not only your forgiveness, but also your blessing that we may continue to grow in the grace and knowledge of Jesus Christ, our Lord and Savior. Make us into your servants, and then we shall be free.

    (silent prayer)

M: And Jesus said: "Do not let your hearts be troubled. Trust in God; trust also in me." In the name of Jesus Christ, you are forgiven!

P: Amen! In the name of Jesus Christ, you are forgiven! Amen!

Eternal God, Judge Almighty, pardon our iniquities. No longer are we eager to do the good you demand. Our fear of you has become an irrational fear of death and we have forgotten your promise of resurrection. If anyone does make the mistake of speaking to us, the only answer we give comes across sharp tongues and through clenched teeth. Our conscience has become clouded with the flattery we have heard and the slander we have spread. Your patience has been rewarded only by our evil disobedience.

Forgive us and enable us to grow through this experience to become the children you would be proud of and in whom you can trust.

(silent prayer)

M: Hear the good news: "Christ died for sins once for all, the righteous for the unrighteous, to bring you to God." In the name of Jesus Christ, you are forgiven!

P: All praises be to the living God! In the name of Jesus Christ, you are forgiven! Amen!

O God, Light of the World and lover of concord; we are certainly sorry for these our misdeeds. Forgive us for those things we have said, thought or done that has caused a brother or sister to stumble and fall. Pick them up and return us to your path. In your hands we still are clay in need of shaping; please remove the rough corners of our lives and shape us to your will.

Come into my heart, Lord Jesus. Pour out your Spirit into my life that I might overflow with your love. Make me a servant and then I shall be free!

(silent prayer)

M: Hear the good news: "It is by grace you have been saved." In the name of Jesus Christ, you are forgiven!

P: We are God's — to the praise of the Lord's eternal glory! In the name of Jesus Christ, you are forgiven! Amen!

O Holy God of grace and glory, in whom mercy grows and finds its beginning. Forgive us and have mercy upon our souls, for we have sinned against the blessings and commandments you placed upon us in your Son Jesus Christ. We spend all of our time looking into heaven and ignore your call to be witnesses in all the earth. We have been more concerned with the times and seasons of your judgment and forgotten that you have called us in wisdom and power to be your agents for salvation in the world around us. We have chosen the easy path of pious proclamations and forgotten the hard path of active Christian love.

(silent prayer)

M: Hear the good news: "As far as the east is from the west, will God remove your sins" In the name of Jesus Christ, you are forgiven!

P: Glory and praise to God who in great might has placed all things under Christ. In the name of Jesus Christ, you are forgiven! Amen!

O God, ruler of all creation; Forgive us, we pray. Because we have made the station of one's life; we have made the nationality of one's heritage; we have made the color of one's skin; we have made the gender of one's body and thoughts; we have taken our human condition as the rule for faith. In judging others we have neglected to consider your judgment upon us. Forgive us, cleanse us of our iniquity and place us once again upon the path you have chosen for our lives.

(silent prayer)

M: Hear the good news: "Everyone who believes in Christ receives forgiveness of sins through Christ's name." In the name of Jesus Christ, you are forgiven!

P: Not in vain have we believed in the power of the gospel. In the name of Jesus Christ, you are forgiven! Amen!

Giving God, you did not even withhold the life of your Son Jesus for our sake. Forgive us, for we require much more of our brothers and sisters, than you do of us. We can reach no agreements, except those to agree to disagree and we have forgotten the power of shared faith and resources. The needy stand among us, as we refuse to cure them. We are far more concerned with the material requirements of human life, than the power with which you touch us to testify to Christ's resurrection.

Forgive us, most merciful God and weld us again into one people for one purpose — your salvation of the world.

> *(silent prayer)*

M: Hear the good news: "We have one who speaks to God in our defense — Jesus Christ who is the atoning sacrifice for our sins." In the name of Jesus Christ, you are forgiven!

P: Thanks and praise be to God! In the name of Jesus Christ, you are forgiven! Amen!

O Jesus, Name above all names, Mighty Redeemer; send your forgiving Spirit upon us, for we have sinned and fallen short of your example and life. We have denied the power of your resurrection and in the presence of the Pilates of this world delivered you up time and time again. In our own thoughts of righteousness we have judged and passed sentence upon our brothers and sisters without a thought for your grace. We have called for the destruction of this sinful world and neglected to consider your call for its redemption. We crave power, even in our servant faith, forgetting your role and place in creation.

Forgive us Lord. Purge our souls of this human impurity that we may once again hope in you.

> *(silent prayer)*

M: Hear the good news: "Your faith which is through Jesus has given you perfect health and blotted out your sins." In the name of Jesus Christ, you are forgiven!

P: "To this we are witnesses, that repentance and forgiveness of sins should be preached and lived in Christ's name to all nations." In the name of Jesus Christ, you are forgiven! Amen!

Shepherding Lord, all we like sheep have gone astray. Forgive us, gather us in your arms and return us to your fold. The wickedness and sins of our lives are many: we have clawed our way onto the shoulders of our sisters to stand above the crowds, we have abused our brothers to enhance our self-image, we have neglected and discarded the children in our homes, our nation, our world to pursue human goals and greed. The only love of our lives has been ourselves.

Forgive us. Help us. Heal us. Save us and return our lives to you that we may center upon your love in all that we do and say.

(silent prayer)

M: Hear the good news: "I am the Good Shepherd; I know my own and my own know me." In the name of Jesus Christ, you are forgiven!

P: "There is salvation in no one else, for there is no other name by which we are saved." In the name of Jesus Christ, you are forgiven! Amen!

Compassionate and loving God; the fruit of your vine has withered upon the branches of our lives. When the world looks to us they have seen only reflections of themselves and not your disciples. Forgive us for those things we have said, thought and done which have caused hate, fear, strife or sin in our brothers and sisters. Prune from our lives this tendency towards sin and give to us the strength of character needed to truly become your disciples.

Remove our withered and broken lives from the fire of your burning judgment and enable the words of your love to abide in us as we do in them.

(silent prayer)

M: And Jesus said: "If you abide in me, and my words abide in you, ask whatever you will, and it shall be done for you." In the name of Jesus Christ, you are forgiven!

P: By this gift of grace God is glorified! In the name of Jesus Christ, you are forgiven! Amen!

Gracious God, giver of love, forgive us for our failings, for we have fallen far short of the life you have shown us in Jesus Christ. We have become so stingy with our love that we have even refused to lay down our lives for ourselves, let alone a friend or stranger. We have neglected, ignored and yes even ridiculed your commandment to love as you have loved.

Through the power of your loving Spirit come into our hearts and in the closeness of our faith family make us once again children of your promise.

(silent prayer)

M: And Jesus said: "You did not choose me, but I chose you that you should go and bear abiding fruit; so that whatever you ask God in my name may be given to you." In the name of Jesus Christ, you are forgiven!

P: **For this is the love of God and by it we know that we are God's children. In the name of Jesus Christ, you are forgiven! Amen!**

Loving God, forgive the inadequacies of our lives, for we have sought to live with you and not under Christ or in and through your love. Like the disciples before us we have not believed the words of your witnesses for in the "reality" of this world it all seems like nonsense. We too have walked away from your empty tomb wondering what has happened, and how we can explain it. We have forgotten or neglected the power of simple faith in you.

Forgive us, and return us to the fold of your loving arms.

(silent prayer)

M: Hear the good news: "Why do you look for the living among the dead?" In the name of Jesus Christ, you are forgiven!

P: **Thanks be to God who has given us the victory in Christ Jesus our Lord! In the name of Jesus Christ, you are forgiven! Amen!**

O Christ, in the fire and persecutions of this world we have found only the temptation to deny and degrade your name and gospel, and not the Spirit to stand firm in our faith. We have rationalized our lives to the point that we no longer believe in your ability and power to act for us in this place. Your angels are no more a part of reality than the characters of comic books or any other mythological hero. In the end we have chosen to obey each other, rather than God. We are truly sorry Jesus; forgive us and in the power of your Spirit enable us to believe and trust in you alone.

    (silent prayer)

M: And Jesus said: "Peace be with you!" In the name of Jesus Christ, you are forgiven!

P: May God be praised on earth and in all the heavenly places. In the name of Jesus Christ, you are forgiven! Amen!

O God, we admit that too often we live on the surface of life. We are afraid of the depths, though we try to hide many things deep within us. We are haunted by the knowledge that we have hurt others by our own selfish acts. We are harassed by the realization that our sense of priorities and laziness have prevented us from responding to situations where we might have made a creative difference. What gets into us, God, to make us miss the mark of our Christian love time after time?

Help us, O God. Make us again to know the peace and joy of believing.

    (silent prayer)

M: Hear the good news: "There is no sin so terrible that God's love cannot forgive." In the name of Jesus Christ, you are forgiven!

P: The mercy of God is everlasting. In the name of Jesus Christ, you are forgiven! Amen!

Saving Shepherd, forgive us, for your voice is so familiar to us that we have begun to take it for granted. You know us even better than we know ourselves, and while no one will ever be able to snatch us out of your loving hands, all we like sheep have gone astray. We have listened to the wolf-songs of Satan and left the security of your fold only to enter the jaws of death in this world.

O Lord Jesus, forgive us and gather us back into that one community of your Body in this world, that we might enter into your world to come.

(silent prayer)

M: Hear the good news: "What God promised to our ancestors, has been fulfilled for us in the raising of Jesus, through whom the forgiveness of sins is proclaimed." In the name of Jesus Christ, you are forgiven!

P: **Praise and glory and wisdom and thanks and honor and power and strength be to God for ever and ever! In the name of Jesus Christ, you are forgiven! Amen!**

Mother and Father God, you know better than we do, and so we confess the failures of our love and the confusion of our lives. We know how often our world is torn by hatred and misunderstanding, and how much this pains you. We know that while we are not personally responsible for all of this dissension, we are guilty of some of it. For there have been times when we have let small differences mushroom into vast difficulties; while at the same time we have ignored important understandings that should have drawn us together in love.

For our tendency to push hate before love, and angry accusations before patient understanding, forgive us, O God.

(silent prayer)

M: And Jesus said: "I make all things new. To the thirsty I will give water without price from the fountain of the water of life." In the name of Jesus Christ, you are forgiven!

P: **Thanks be to God who preserves all who love the Lord Jesus. In the name of Jesus Christ, you are forgiven! Amen!**

O Jesus, forgive us. We have tried to disassociate love from obedience and so make your love into only some kind of warm inner feeling, while seeing obedience as only something we must require of others ... and not of ourselves. We have felt the touch of our Counselor, however we have refused to remember all that the Holy Spirit has taught us about you. To our scientific minds the fact of your resurrection is not enough to empower our belief. We so dearly want proof, and when we are given it, we attempt either to discredit that truth or the one who brought it.

Lamb of God, forgive us and spare us, that we might know the real and true presence of your peace.

    (silent prayer)

M: And Jesus said: "Do not let your hearts be troubled, and do not be afraid." In the name of Jesus Christ, you are forgiven!

P: In the name of Jesus Christ, you are forgiven! Amen!

Precious Jesus, forgive us. Time and time again your servant witnesses have entered our fellowship and loudly proclaimed your gospel. Each and every time we have heard them we ignored their message, ridiculed their person, distorted their facts, and simply refused to believe them. We have refused to go into the world for you, we even balk at the idea of speaking of you with the person next to us in the pew. Our condemnation is sure.

Forgive us, O Lord and save us for your work.

    (silent prayer)

M: Hear the good news: "Whoever believes and is baptized will be saved." In the name of Jesus Christ, you are forgiven!

P: Praise to the Lord, the Almighty, the King of Creation! In the name of Jesus Christ, you are forgiven! Amen!

Prayers of Dedication
For Easter

O God, guide of the meek and helper of all persons, we come now to bring these our gifts and lives to you alone, that the work of your kingdom might excel and expand into all the world. **Amen.**

Powerful God, resurrector and life giver; before you we are nothing at all, and yet in faith we have come to bring these gifts and our lives in humble adoration to you and your kingdom; accept them and bless us to your work of love. **Amen.**

Adonai, source of all that was, is and shall be, we have brought this money and our lives to you today in simple trust, believing that you do know what needs to be done. Take it and use us as only you can. **Amen.**

Precisely because you first gave the life of your one and only Son for us, we gladly surrender these first fruits of our lives to the blessings of your work. To you, O Lord, who through birth has given us life and new life, we dedicate this money, for we know that whatever we do, we do it to you. **Amen.**

O God, maker of all things, we bring these offerings of our money and lives to you today in recognition of the many gifts you have blessed us with, most especially Jesus Christ, and we pray that through the lives we lead before you this week we might be made worthy of your many blessings. **Amen.**

God has raised Jesus to life, and we have brought these tithes and our lives today in witness to this fact. Please take and use them and us, O Lord, as only you can. **Amen.**

Thank you, God, for the beauty of Spring and the cross. We are reminded that Jesus is alive and helping to make our lives beautiful. Thank you, for sharing Jesus with us. Thank you, for choosing us to carry on the work and life of Jesus. We bring our offerings today to help in that work. Bless them so that they can do good in our town and around the world. Help us to be better helpers every day. **Amen.**

High and Holy God, we who are your children only by the gift of your one and only Son Jesus Christ bring these offerings into your presence today, that in the work of your will they might become blessed to your kingdom. **Amen.**

Dear Jesus, generous provider of love and life, we bring these gifts of our lives in humble tithe and response to your great and perfect gift to us. **Amen.**

Glorious God of the loving heart, we come now in prayer seeking your blessing upon these gifts both personal and monetary, that the changes they bring for your kingdom might be reflected in the lives they represent. **Amen.**

Almighty giver of all good gifts, we bring these gifts and our lives in recognition of our faith responsibilities in Christ to you and your kingdom. Take, bless them and use us for your honor and glory. **Amen.**

Jesus, Savior and pure deliverer, these gifts and our lives we bring in humble adoration to the work and will of your kingdom now on earth and eternally in heaven. **Amen.**

Christ Almighty, we bring this offering of the first fruits of our lives in loving tithe seeking nothing for ourselves, but looking rather toward your kingdom and your continued glory and honor. **Amen.**

O God of this day and all time, out of the immeasurable love you have blessed us with, we come into your presence today with these gifts of our lives. Bless them to the mighty work of your saints in the world now and in the kingdom to come. **Amen.**

Risen and Ascended Christ, by the power of your life in us we have brought these our tithes to you today. Accept them and use us in your ministry as witnesses to your kingdom. **Amen.**

O Lord God, whose glory lights the new heaven and new earth, we humbly bow in your almighty presence as we bring these tithes and offer them to you in the name of the Lamb, that your honor and power might glorify all creation. **Amen.**

O God, whose people we are, we dedicate these gifts to your mighty name; that dwelling with us you might find acceptable vessels and means for your blessings and love in this world. **Amen.**

O Great and Mighty God, whose Word was upon creation, is with us now and will echo through the vaults of time itself, receive these gifts of money in the spirit they have been offered and bless the lives here represented, even as they have sought to bless you. We pray this and all things in the name, presence and power of your one and only Son, Jesus Christ. **Amen.**

O Giver of Life, as we offer our money to you, help us also to be able to offer you ourselves. We know that your gifts cannot be hoarded, that they are for spending. Help and guide us in this time of offering to discover how we need to spend ourselves today. **Amen.**

Creative God, in thanks and praise we offer back to you now our lives which you have gifted us with, and we pray that the blessings you have touched us with and that we return to you now, might be used for your kingdom as only you wish. **Amen.**

Living God, in whose house we have gathered and in whose love we live each day, accept and bless these firstfruits of our lives to the continuing work of your glorious reign. **Amen.**

Resurrecting God, in lifting up Jesus Christ you have given us that immeasurable gift of hope in eternal life, and as we come today bringing our tithes before you we do so in response to that one gift of your everlasting love, asking only that you take them and use us as only you can. **Amen.**

Gospel
Dialogues

Ash Wednesday
From Matthew 6:1-6, 16-21

Reader 1: Beware of practicing your piety before others in order to be seen by them; for then you have no reward from your Father in heaven. So whenever you give alms, do not sound a trumpet before you, as the hypocrites do in the synagogues and in the streets, so that they may be praised by others. Truly I tell you, they have received their reward.

Reader 2: But when you give alms, do not let your left hand know what your right hand is doing, so that your alms may be done in secret, and your Father who sees in secret will reward you.

Reader 1: And whenever you pray, do not be like the hypocrites, for they love to stand and pray in the synagogues and at the street corners, so that they may be seen by others. Truly I tell you, they have received their reward.

Reader 2: But whenever you pray, go into your room and shut the door and pray to your Father who is in secret, and your Father who sees in secret will reward you.

Reader 1: And whenever you fast, do not look dismal, like the hypocrites, for they disfigure their faces so as to show others that they are fasting. Truly I tell you, they have received their reward.

Reader 2: But when you fast, put oil on your head and wash your face, so that your fasting may be seen not by others but by your Father who is in secret, and your Father who sees in secret will reward you.

Reader 1: Do not store up for yourselves treasures on earth, where moth and rust consume and where thieves break in and steal, but store up for yourselves treasures in heaven, where neither moth nor rust consumes and where thieves do not break in and steal.

Reader 2: For where your treasure is, there your heart will be also.

Lent 1
From Matthew 4:1-11

Reader 1: Then Jesus was led up by the Spirit into the wilderness to be tempted by the devil. Jesus fasted forty days and forty nights, and afterwards was famished. The tempter came and said to Jesus,

Reader 2: "If you are the Son of God, command these stones to become loaves of bread."

Reader 1: But Jesus answered,

People: "It is written, 'One does not live by bread alone, but by every word that comes from the mouth of God.'"

Reader 1: Then the devil took Jesus to the holy city and placed him on the pinnacle of the temple, saying,

Reader 2: "If you are the Son of God, throw yourself down, for it is written, 'He will command his angels concerning you,' and 'On their hands they will bear you up, so that you will not dash your foot against a stone.'"

Reader 1: Jesus replied,

People: "Again it is written, 'Do not put the Lord your God to the test.'"

Reader 1: Again, the devil took Jesus to a very high mountain and showed him all the kingdoms of the world and their splendor; and said,

Reader 2: "All these I will give you, if you will fall down and worship me."

Reader 1: To which Jesus replied,

People: "Away with you, Satan! for it is written, 'Worship the Lord your God, and serve only him.'"

Reader 1: Then the devil left Jesus, and suddenly angels came and waited on him.

Lent 2
From Mark 8:31-38

Reader: Then Jesus began to teach them that the Son of Man must undergo great suffering, and be rejected by the elders, the chief priests, and the scribes, and be killed, and after three days rise again. He said all this quite openly. And Peter took him aside and began to rebuke him. But turning and looking at his disciples, he rebuked Peter and said,

People: "Get behind me, Satan! For you are setting your mind not on divine things but on human things."

Reader: Jesus then called the crowd with his disciples, and said to them,

People: "If any want to become my followers, let them deny themselves and take up their cross and follow me. For those who want to save their life will lose it, and those who lose their life for my sake, and for the sake of the gospel, will save it. For what will it profit them to gain the whole world and forfeit their life? Indeed, what can they give in return for their life? Those who are ashamed of me and of my words in this adulterous and sinful generation, of them the Son of Man will also be ashamed when he comes in the glory of his Father with the holy angels."

Lent 3
From John 2:13-22

Reader 1: The Passover of the Jews was near, and Jesus went up to Jerusalem. In the temple he found people selling cattle, sheep, and doves, and the money changers seated at their tables. Making a whip of cords, Jesus drove all of them out of the temple, both the sheep and the cattle. He also poured out the coins of the money changers and overturned their tables. Jesus then told those who were selling the doves,

Reader 2: "Take these things out of here! Stop making my Father's house a marketplace!"

Reader 1: At this point the disciples remembered that it was written, "Zeal for your house will consume me." The Jews then said to him,

People: "What sign can you show us for doing this?"

Reader 2: "Destroy this temple, and in three days I will raise it up."

People: "This temple has been under construction for forty-six years, and will you raise it up in three days?"

Reader 1: But Jesus was speaking of the temple of his body. After he was raised from the dead, the disciples remembered that Jesus had said this; and they believed the scripture and the word that had been spoken.

Lent 4
From Luke 15:1-3, 11b-32

Reader 1: Now all the tax collectors and sinners were coming near to listen to him. And the Pharisees and the scribes were grumbling and saying, "This fellow welcomes sinners and eats with them." So Jesus told them this parable: "There was a man who had two sons. The younger of them said to his father,

People: 'Father, give me the share of the property that will belong to me.'

Reader 1: "So the Father divided his property between them. A few days later the younger son gathered all he had and traveled to a distant country, and there he squandered his property in dissolute living. When he had spent everything, a severe famine took place throughout that country, and he began to be in need. So he went and hired himself out to one of the citizens of that country, who sent him to his fields to feed the pigs. He would gladly have filled himself with the pods that the pigs were eating; and no one gave him anything. But when he came to himself he said,

People: 'How many of my father's hired hands have bread enough and to spare, but here I am dying of hunger! I will get up and go to my father, and I will say to him, "Father, I have sinned against heaven and before you; I am no longer worthy to be called your son; treat me like one of your hired hands."'

Reader 1: "So the young man set off and went to his father. But while he was still far off, his father saw him and was filled with compassion; he ran and put his arms around him and kissed him. Then the son said to him,

People: 'Father, I have sinned against heaven and before you; I am no longer worthy to be called your son.'

Reader 1: "To which the father responded by saying to his slaves,

Reader 2: 'Quickly, bring out a robe — the best one — and put it on him; put a ring on his finger and sandals on his feet. And get the fatted calf and kill it, and let us eat and celebrate; for this son of mine was dead and is alive again; he was lost and is found!'

Reader 1: "And they began to celebrate. Now the elder son was in the field; and when he came and approached the house, he heard music and dancing. He called one of the slaves and asked what was going on. He replied,

Reader 2: 'Your brother has come, and your father has killed the fatted calf, because he has got him back safe and sound.'

Reader 1: "Then the elder son became angry and refused to go in. His father came out and began to plead with him. But he answered his father,

People: 'Listen! For all these years I have been working like a slave for you, and I have never disobeyed your command; yet you have never given me even a young goat so that I might celebrate with my friends. But when this son of yours came back, who has devoured your property with prostitutes, you killed the fatted calf for him!'

Reader 1: "To which the father replied,

Reader 2: 'Son, you are always with me, and all that is mine is yours. But we had to celebrate and rejoice, because this brother of yours was dead and has come to life; he was lost and has been found.'"

Lent 5

From John 12:20-33

Reader 1: Now among those who went up to worship at the festival were some Greeks. They came to Philip, who was from Bethsaida in Galilee, and said to him,

People: "Sir, we wish to see Jesus."

Reader 1: Philip went and told Andrew; then Andrew and Philip went and told Jesus. Jesus answered them,

Reader 2: "The hour has come for the Son of Man to be glorified. Very truly, I tell you, unless a grain of wheat falls into the earth and dies, it remains just a single grain; but if it dies, it bears much fruit. Those who love their life lose it, and those who hate their life in this world will keep it for eternal life. Whoever serves me must follow me, and where I am, there will my servant be also. Whoever serves me, the Father will honor. Now my soul is troubled. And what should I say — 'Father, save me from this hour'? No, it is for this reason that I have come to this hour. Father, glorify your name."

Reader 1: Then a voice came from heaven,

Choir: "I have glorified it, and I will glorify it again."

Reader 1: The crowd standing there heard it and said that it was thunder. Others said, "An angel has spoken to him." And so, Jesus answered,

Reader 2: "This voice has come for your sake, not for mine. Now is the judgment of this world; now the ruler of this world will be driven out. And I, when I am lifted up from the earth, will draw all people to myself."

Reader 1: Jesus said this to indicate the kind of death he was to die.

Palm Sunday
From Matthew 21:1-11

Reader 1: When Jesus and the disciples drew near to Jerusalem and came to Bethany, to the Mount of Olives, he sent two disciples on ahead, saying to them,

Reader 2: "Go into the village opposite you, and immediately you will find a donkey tied, and a colt with it, untie them and bring them to me. If anyone says anything to you, you shall say, 'The Lord has need of them' and they will be sent immediately."

Reader 1: This took place to fulfill what was spoken by the prophet,

People: "Tell the daughter of Zion, Behold, your King is coming to you, humble and mounted on a donkey and on a colt, the foal of a donkey."

Reader 1: The disciples went and did as Jesus had directed them, they brought the donkey and the colt, and put their garments on them, and Jesus sat there. Most of the crowd spread their garments on the road, and others cut branches from the trees and spread them on the road. And the crowds that went before Jesus and those that followed him, shouted,

People: "Hosanna to the Son of David! Blessed is the one who comes in the name of the Lord! Hosanna in the highest!"

Reader 1: And when Jesus entered Jerusalem, all the city was stirred, saying,

Reader 2: "Who is this?"

Reader 1: And the crowds said,

People: "This is the prophet Jesus from Nazareth of Galilee."

Maundy Thursday

From John 13:1-17, 31-35

Reader 1: Now before the festival of the Passover, Jesus knew that his hour had come to depart from this world and go to the Father. Having loved his own who were in the world, he loved them to the end. The devil had already put it into the heart of Judas son of Simon Iscariot to betray him.

Reader 2: And during supper Jesus, knowing that the Father had given all things into his hands, and that he had come from God and was going to God, got up from the table, took off his outer robe, and tied a towel around himself. Then he poured water into a basin and began to wash the disciples' feet and to wipe them with the towel that was tied around him. Jesus came to Simon Peter, who said to him,

People: "Lord, are you going to wash my feet?"

Reader 1: And Jesus answered,

Reader 2: "You do not know now what I am doing, but later you will understand."

People: "You will never wash my feet."

Reader 2: "Unless I wash you, you have no share with me."

Reader 1: Which is why Simon Peter said to him,

People: "Lord, not my feet only but also my hands and my head!"

Reader 2: "One who has bathed does not need to wash, except for the feet, but is entirely clean. And you are clean, though not all of you."

Reader 1: Jesus knew who was to betray him; for this reason he had said, "Not all of you are clean." After Jesus had washed their feet, had put on his robe, and had returned to the table, he said to them,

Reader 2: "Do you know what I have done to you? You call me Teacher and Lord — and you are right, for that is what I am. So if I, your Lord and Teacher, have washed your feet, you also ought to wash one another's feet. For I have set you an example, that you also should do as I have done to you. Very truly, I tell you, servants are not greater than their master, nor are messengers greater than the one who sent them. If you know these things, you are blessed if you do them."

Reader 1: When Judas had gone out to do that thing which was his alone, Jesus said,

Reader 2: "Now the Son of Man has been glorified, and God has been glorified in him. If God has been glorified in him, God will also glorify him in himself and will glorify him at once. Little children, I am with you only a little longer. You will look for me; and as I said to the Jews so now I say to you, 'Where I am going, you cannot come.' I give you a new commandment, that you love one another. Just as I have loved you, you also should love one another. By this everyone will know that you are my disciples, if you have love for one another."

Good Friday
From John 18:1—19:42

Reader 1: After Jesus had spoken these words, he went out with his disciples across the Kidron valley to a place where there was a garden, which he and his disciples entered. Now Judas, who betrayed him, also knew the place, because Jesus often met there with his disciples. So Judas brought a detachment of soldiers together with police from the chief priests and the Pharisees, and they came there with lanterns and torches and weapons. Then Jesus, knowing all that was to happen to him, came forward and asked them,

Reader 2: "Whom are you looking for?"

Reader 1: Those with Judas answered,

Choir: "Jesus of Nazareth."

Reader 2: "I am he."

Reader 1: Now Judas, who betrayed him, was standing with them and when Jesus said to them, "I am he," they stepped back and fell to the ground. So, again Jesus asked them,

Reader 2: "Whom are you looking for?"

Choir: "Jesus of Nazareth."

Reader 2: "I told you that I am he. So if you are looking for me, let these men go."

Reader 1: This was to fulfill the word that he had spoken, "I did not lose a single one of those whom you gave me." Then Simon Peter, who had a sword, drew it, struck the high priest's slave, and cut off his right ear. The slave's name was Malchus. Jesus said to Peter,

Reader 2: "Put your sword back into its sheath. Am I not to drink the cup that the Father has given me?"

Reader 1: So the soldiers, their officer, and the Jewish police arrested Jesus and bound him. First they took him to Annas, who was the father-in-law of Caiaphas, the high priest that year. Caiaphas was the one who had advised the Jews that it was better to have one person die for the people. Simon Peter and another disciple followed Jesus. Since that disciple was known to the high priest, he went with Jesus into the courtyard of the high priest, but Peter was standing outside at the gate. So the other disciple, who was known to the high priest, went out, spoke to the woman who guarded the gate, and brought Peter in. The woman said to Peter,

Choir: "You are not also one of this man's disciples, are you?"

Reader 1: To which Peter replied,

People: "I am not."

Reader 1: Now the slaves and the police had made a charcoal fire because it was cold, and they were standing around it and warming themselves. Peter also was standing with them and warming himself. Then the high priest questioned Jesus about his disciples and about his teaching. Jesus answered,

Reader 2: "I have spoken openly to the world; I have always taught in synagogues and in the temple, where all the Jews come together. I have said nothing in secret. Why do you ask me? Ask those who heard what I said to them; they know what I said."

Reader 1: When he had said this, one of the police standing nearby struck Jesus on the face, saying, "Is that how you answer the high priest?"

Reader 2: "If I have spoken wrongly, testify to the wrong. But if I have spoken rightly, why do you strike me?"

Reader 1: Then Annas sent him bound to Caiaphas the high priest. Now Simon Peter was standing and warming himself. They asked him,

Choir: "You are not also one of his disciples, are you?"

Reader 1: Again Peter denied it and said,

People: "I am not."

Reader 1: Then one of the slaves of the high priest, a relative of the man whose ear Peter had cut off, asked,

Choir: "Did I not see you in the garden with him?"

Reader 1: Again Peter denied it, and at that moment the cock crowed. Then they took Jesus from Caiaphas to Pilate's headquarters. It was early in the morning. They themselves did not enter the headquarters, so as to avoid ritual defilement and to be able to eat the Passover. So Pilate went out to them and said,

Choir: "What accusation do you bring against this man?"

Reader 1: The Jews who had brought Jesus answered,

People: "If this man were not a criminal, we would not have handed him over to you."

Reader 1: Pilate told them that they should judge Jesus according to their own Law and the Jews reminded Pilate that under the occupation they were not allowed to put anyone to death. (This was to fulfill what Jesus had said when he indicated the kind of death he was to die.) Then Pilate entered the headquarters again, summoned Jesus, and asked him,

Choir: "Are you the King of the Jews?"

Reader 2: "Do you ask this on your own, or did others tell you about me?"

Choir: "I am not a Jew, am I? Your own nation and the chief priests have handed you over to me. What have you done?"

Reader 2: "My kingdom is not from this world. If my kingdom were from this world, my followers would be fighting to keep me from being handed over to the Jews. But as it is, my kingdom is not from here."

Choir: "So you are a king?"

Reader 2: "You say that I am a king. For this I was born, and for this I came into the world, to testify to the truth. Everyone who belongs to the truth listens to my voice."

Reader 1: After asking Jesus, "What is truth?" Pilate went out to the Jews again and told them,

Choir: "I find no case against him. But you have a custom that I release someone for you at the Passover. Do you want me to release for you the King of the Jews?"

Reader 1: As one the people shouted in reply,

People: "Not this man, but Barabbas!"

Reader 1: Now Barabbas was a bandit. Then Pilate took Jesus and had him flogged. And the soldiers wove a crown of thorns and put it on his head, and they dressed him in a purple robe. They kept coming up to him, saying, "Hail, King of the Jews!" and striking him on the face. Pilate went out again and said to them,

Choir: "Look, I am bringing him out to you to let you know that I find no case against him."

Reader 1: So Jesus came out, wearing the crown of thorns and the purple robe. Pilate said to them,

Choir: "Here is the man!"

Reader 1: When the chief priests and the police saw him, they shouted,

People: "Crucify him! Crucify him!"

Choir: "Take him yourselves and crucify him; I find no case against this Jesus."

Reader 1: Now the Jews answered Pilate saying, "We have a law, and according to that law he ought to die because he has claimed to be the Son of God." When Pilate heard this, he was more afraid than ever and entered his headquarters again and asked Jesus,

Choir: "Where are you from?"

Reader 1: (pause) But Jesus gave him no answer.   And so, Pilate said to him,

Choir: "Do you refuse to speak to me? Do you not know that I have power to release you, and power to crucify you?"

Reader 2: "You would have no power over me unless it had been given you from above, therefore the one who handed me over to you is guilty of a greater sin."

Reader 1: From then on Pilate tried to release Jesus, but the Jews continued to cry out, "If you release this man, you are no friend of the emperor. Everyone who claims to be a king sets himself against the emperor." When Pilate heard these words, he brought Jesus outside and sat on the judge's bench at a place called The Stone Pavement. Now it was the day of Preparation for the Passover; and it was about noon. Pilate said to the Jews,

Choir: "Here is your King!"

Reader 1: And the people again cried out as one,

People: "Away with him! Away with him! Crucify him!"

Reader 1: Pilate really wanted to know, and so again he asked

Choir: "Shall I crucify your King?"

People: "We have no king but the emperor."

Reader 1: Then Pilate handed Jesus over to them to be crucified. So they took Jesus; and carrying the cross by himself, Jesus went out to what is called The Place of the Skull, which in Hebrew is called Golgotha. There they crucified Jesus, and with him two others, one on either side. Pilate also had an inscription written and put on the cross. It read, "Jesus of Nazareth, the King of the Jews." Many of the Jews read this inscription, because the place where Jesus was crucified was near the city; and it was written in Hebrew, in Latin, and in Greek. When the soldiers had crucified Jesus, they took his clothes and divided them into four parts, one for each soldier. They also took his tunic; now the tunic was seamless, woven in one piece from the top. So they said to one another, "Let us not tear it, but cast lots for it to see who will get it." This was to fulfill what the scripture says, "They divided my clothes among themselves, and for my clothing they cast lots." And that is what the soldiers did. Meanwhile, standing near the cross of Jesus were his mother, and his mother's sister, Mary the wife of Clopas, and Mary Magdalene. When Jesus saw his mother and the disciple whom he loved standing beside her, he said to his mother,

Reader 2: "Woman, here is your son."

Reader 1: Then Jesus said to the disciple,

Reader 2: "Here is your mother."

Reader 1: And from that hour the disciple took her into his own home. After this, when Jesus knew that all was now finished, (in order to fulfill the scripture) he said,

Reader 2: "I am thirsty."

Reader 1: Now, a jar full of sour wine was standing there. So they put a sponge full of the wine on a branch of hyssop and held it to his mouth. When Jesus had received the wine, he said,

Reader 2: "It is finished."

Reader 1: Then Jesus bowed his head and gave up his spirit. (pause) Since it was the day of Preparation, the Jews did not want the bodies left on the cross during the Sabbath, especially because that Sabbath was a day of great solemnity. So they asked Pilate to have the legs of the crucified men broken and the bodies removed. Then the soldiers came and broke the legs of the first and of the other who had been crucified with him. But when they came to Jesus and saw that he was already dead, they did not break his legs. Instead, one of the soldiers pierced his side with a spear, and at once blood and water came out. (He who saw this has testified so that you also may believe. His testimony is true, and he knows that he tells the truth.)

Reader 2: These things occurred so that the scripture might be fulfilled, "None of his bones shall be broken." And again another passage of scripture says, "They will look on the one whom they have pierced." After these things, Joseph of Arimathea, who was a disciple of Jesus, though a secret one because of his fear of the Jews, asked Pilate to let him take away the body of Jesus. Pilate gave him permission; so he came and removed his body. Nicodemus, who had at first come to Jesus by night, also came, bringing a mixture of myrrh and aloes, weighing about a hundred pounds.

Reader 1: They took the body of Jesus and wrapped it with the spices in linen cloths, according to the burial custom of the Jews. Now there was a garden in the place where he was crucified, and in the garden there was a new tomb in which no one had ever been laid. And so, because it was the Jewish day of Preparation, and the tomb was nearby, (with Reader 2) they laid Jesus there.

Easter

From Luke 24:1-2

Reader 1: But on the first day of the week, at early dawn, they came to the tomb, taking the spices that they had prepared. They found the stone rolled away from the tomb, but when they went in, they did not find the body. While they were perplexed about this, suddenly two men in dazzling clothes stood beside them. The women were terrified and bowed their faces to the ground, but the men said to them,

Reader 2: "Why do you look for the living among the dead? He is not here, but has risen. Remember how he told you, while he was still in Galilee, that the Son of Man must be handed over to sinners, and be crucified, and on the third day rise again."

Reader 1: Then the women remembered Jesus' words, and returning from the tomb, they told all this to the eleven and to all the rest. Now it was Mary Magdalene, Joanna, Mary the mother of James, and the other women with them who told this to the apostles. But these words seemed to them an idle tale, and they did not believe them.

Reader 2: But Peter got up and ran to the tomb; stooping and looking in, he saw the linen cloths by themselves; then he went home, amazed at what had happened.